AF614937

SEE IT GROW!
See a Pineapple Grow
by Kirsten Chang
BLASTOFF! READERS
1
BELLWETHER MEDIA • MINNEAPOLIS, MN

Blastoff! Readers are carefully developed by literacy experts to build reading stamina and move students toward fluency by combining standards-based content with developmentally appropriate text.

Level 1 provides the most support through repetition of high-frequency words, light text, predictable sentence patterns, and strong visual support.

Level 2 offers early readers a bit more challenge through varied sentences, increased text load, and text-supportive special features.

Level 3 advances early-fluent readers toward fluency through increased text load, less reliance on photos, advancing concepts, longer sentences, and more complex special features.

★ **Blastoff! Universe**

Reading Level

Grade K

Grades 1–3

Grade 4

This edition first published in 2024 by Bellwether Media, Inc.

Library of Congress Cataloging-in-Publication Data

LC record for See a Pineapple Grow available at: https://lccn.loc.gov/2023000647

Editor: Elizabeth Neuenfeldt Designer: Brittany McIntosh

Printed in the United States of America, North Mankato, MN.

Table of Contents

Juicy Fruit

We eat pineapple. This juicy fruit grows in the **tropics**.

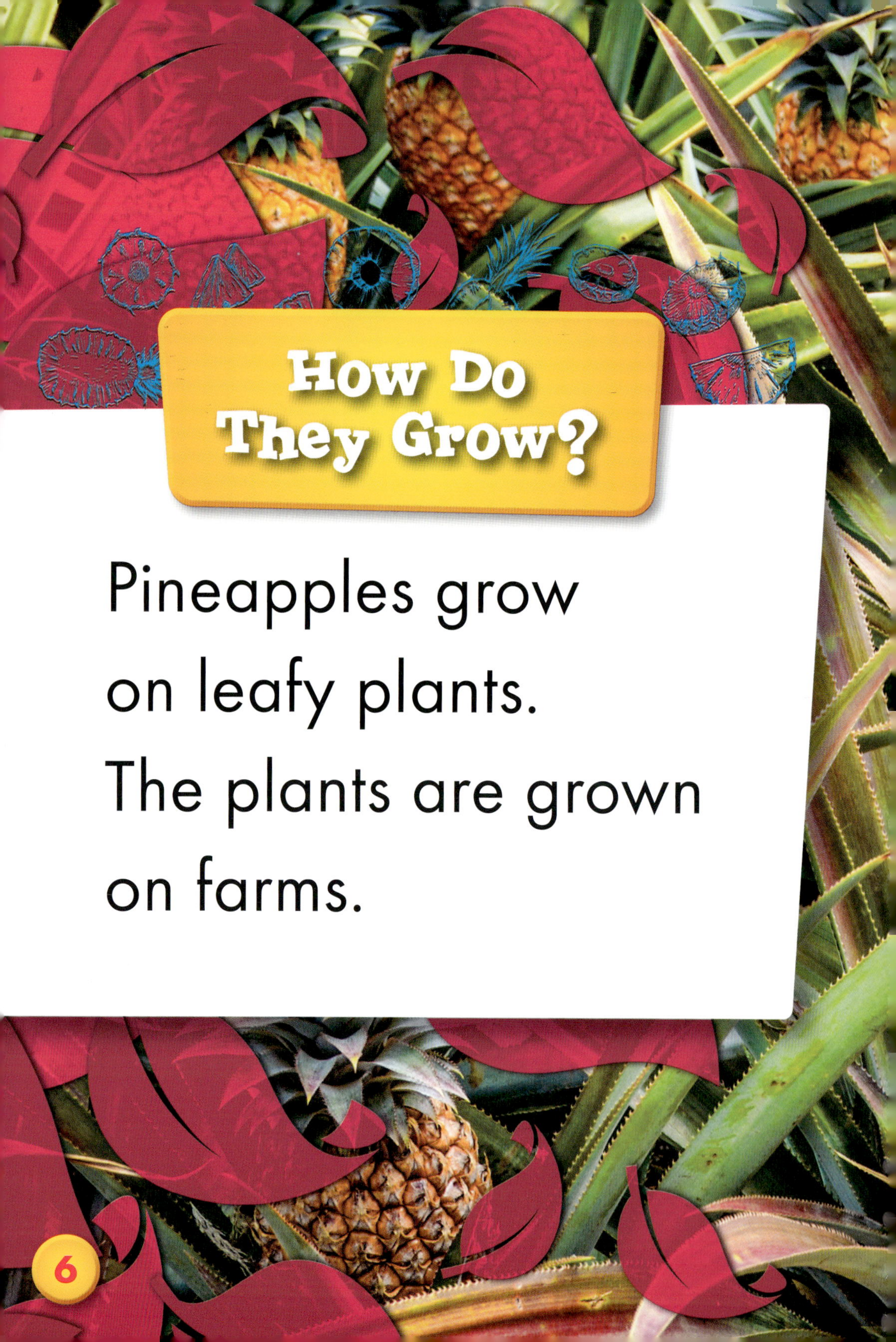

How Do They Grow?

Pineapples grow on leafy plants. The plants are grown on farms.

The plants grow from **cuttings** of pineapples.

cutting

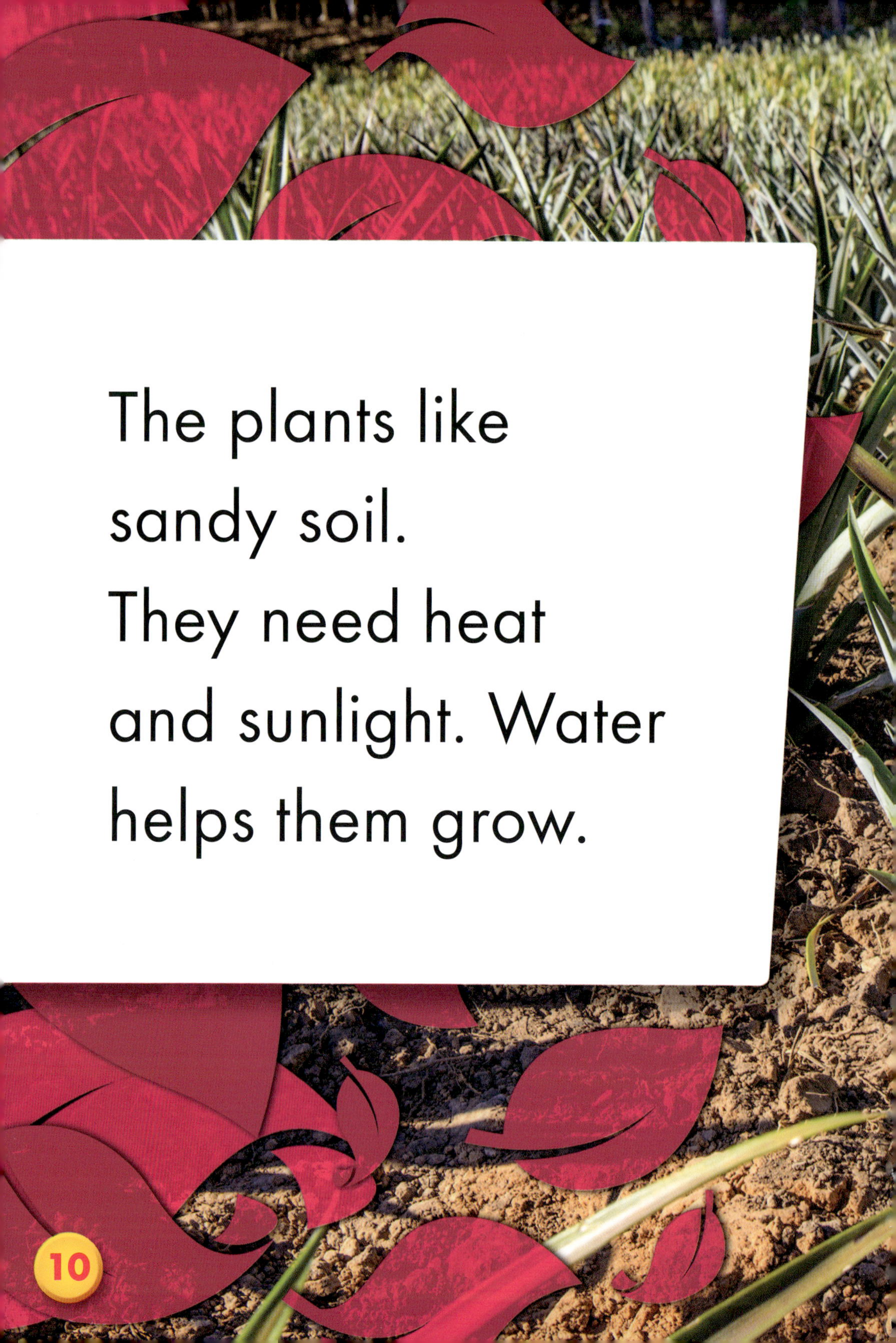

The plants like sandy soil. They need heat and sunlight. Water helps them grow.

Needed to Grow
sandy soil
heat and sunlight
water

The plants grow slowly. In around two years, flowers begin to grow.

flowers

The flowers **fuse** together. They form a small pineapple. Soon, it will be **ripe**!

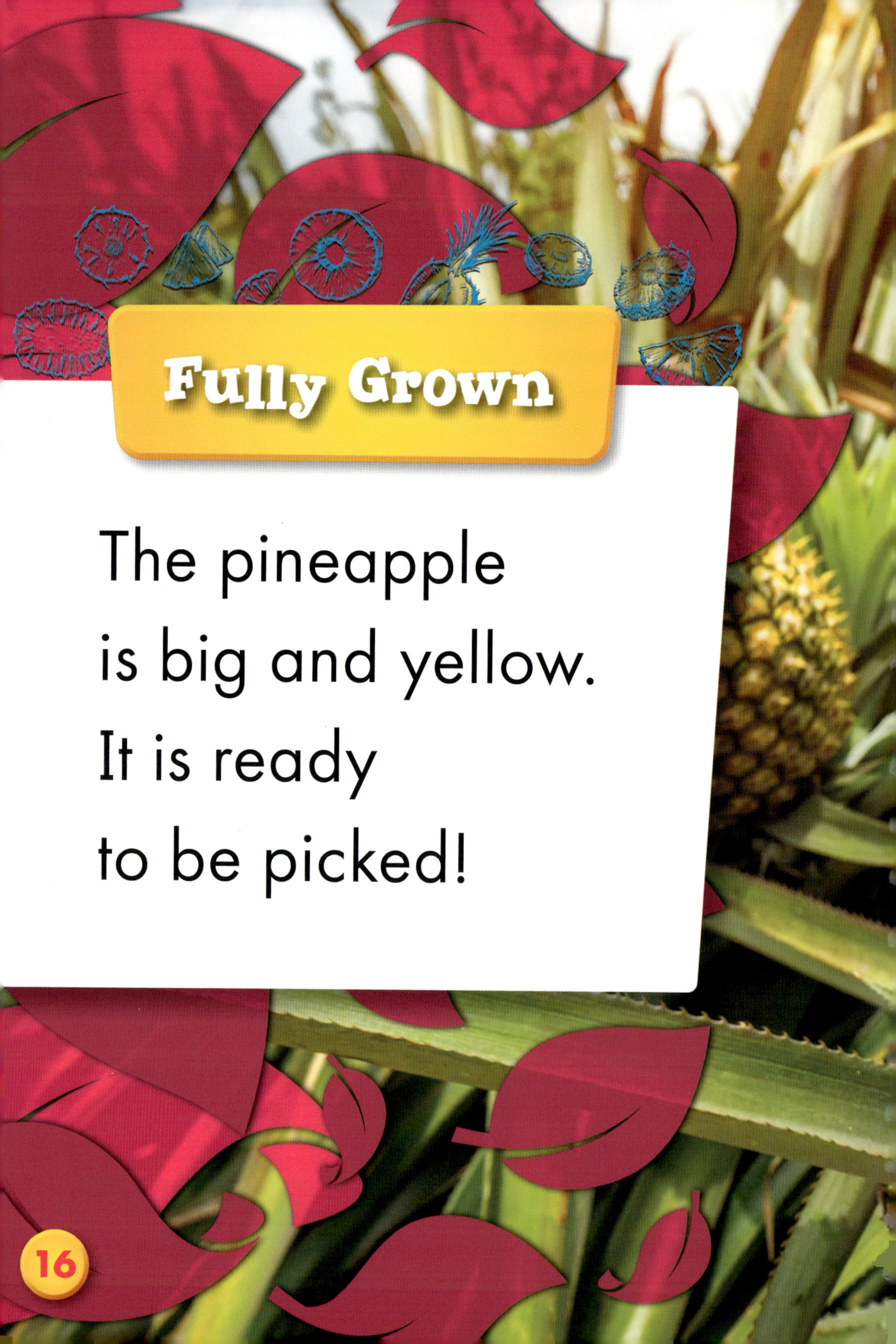

Fully Grown

The pineapple
is big and yellow.
It is ready
to be picked!

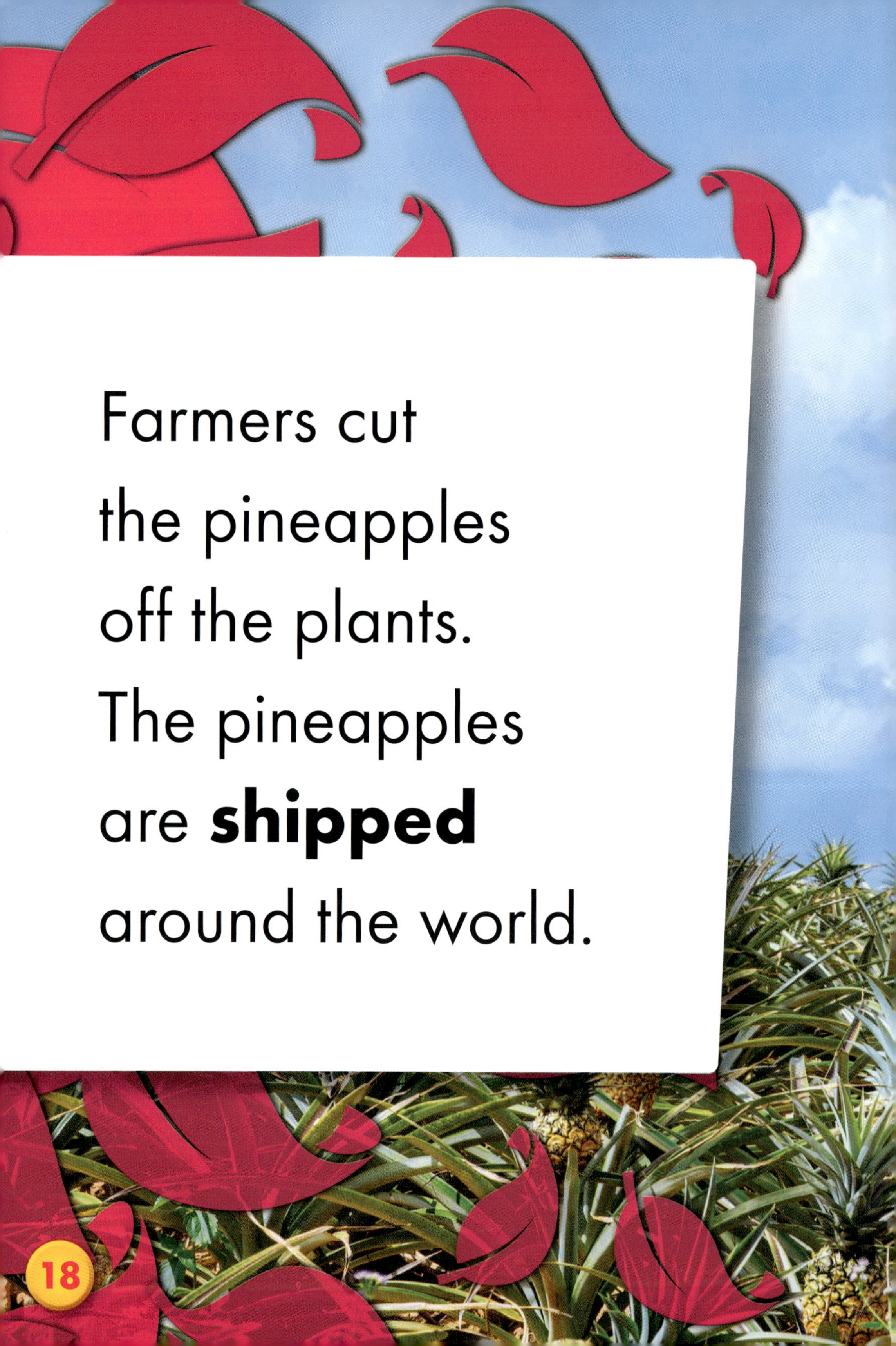

Farmers cut
the pineapples
off the plants.
The pineapples
are **shipped**
around the world.

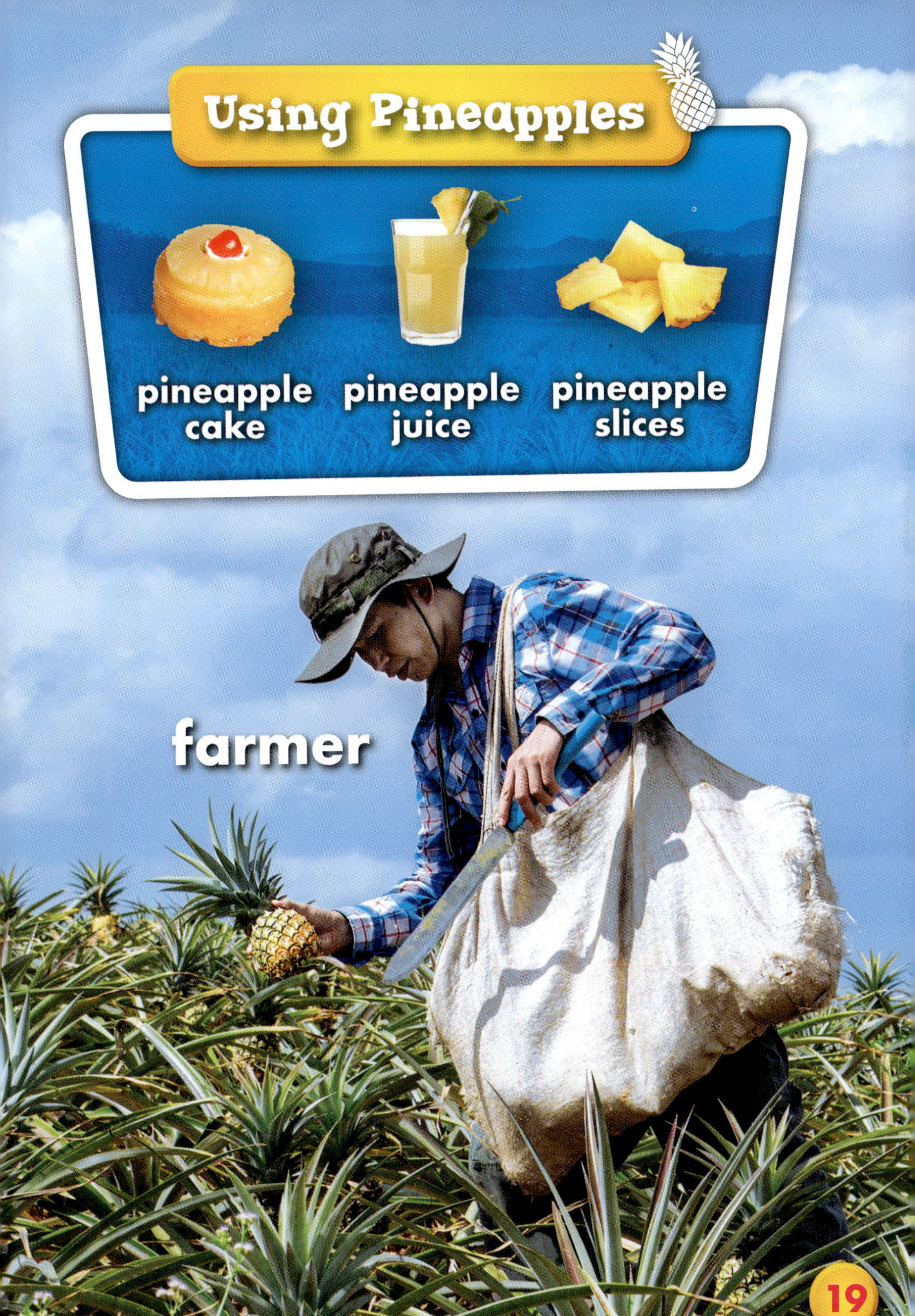
Using Pineapples
pineapple cake
pineapple juice
pineapple slices
farmer

We slice a pineapple to eat. It is a sweet treat!

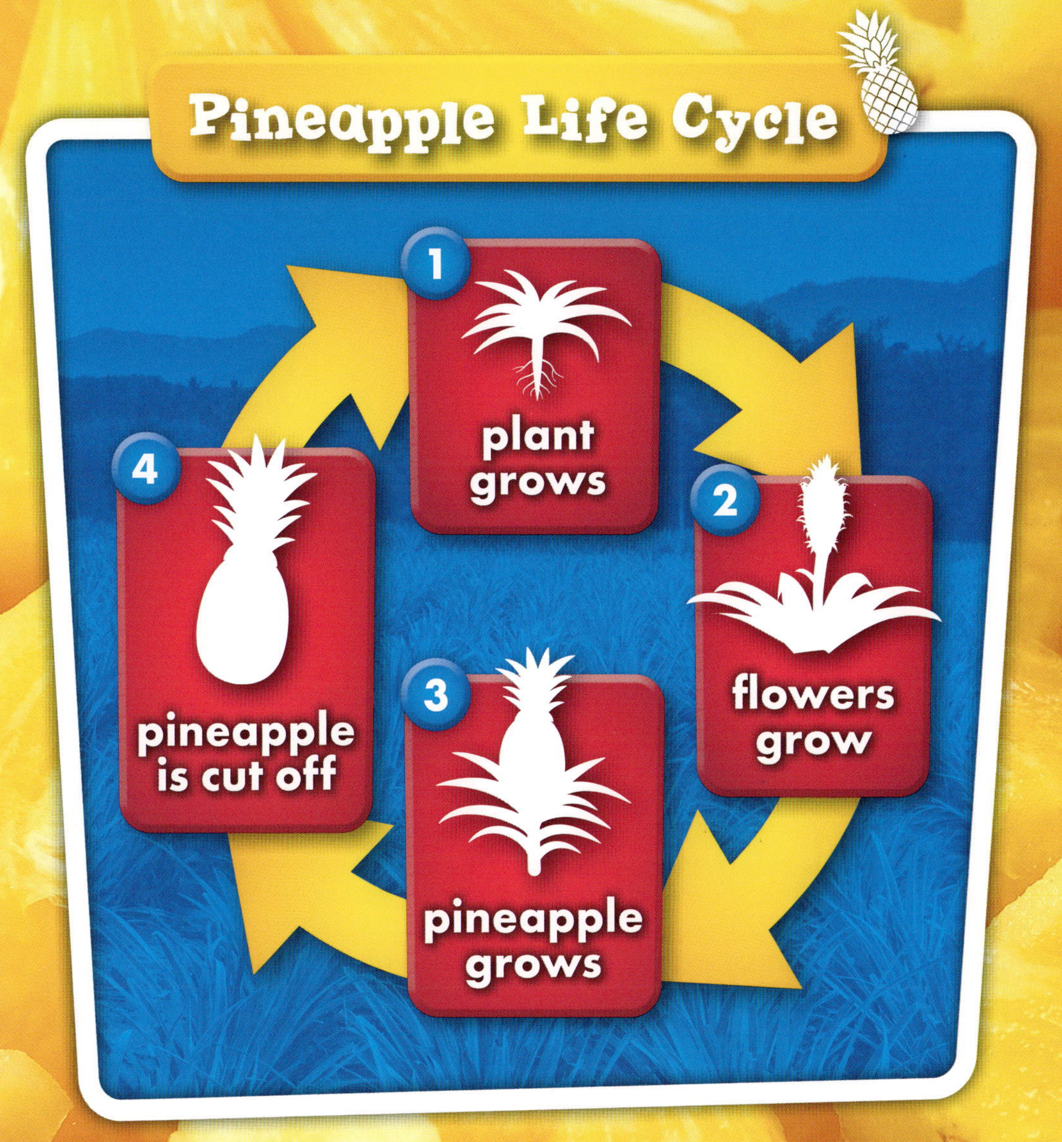
Pineapple Life Cycle
1
plant grows
2
flowers grow
3
pineapple grows
4
pineapple is cut off

Glossary

cuttings

pieces of plants used to grow more plants

shipped

sent from one place to another

fuse

join or combine

tropics

hot parts of the world

ripe

fully grown

To Learn More

AT THE LIBRARY

Bassier, Emma. *Pineapples.* Minneapolis, Minn.: Abdo, 2021.

Chang, Kirsten. *See a Banana Grow.* Minneapolis, Minn.: Bellwether Media, 2023.

Sterling, Charlie W. *Watermelon.* Minneapolis, Minn.: Jump!, 2023.

ON THE WEB

FACTSURFER

Factsurfer.com gives you a safe, fun way to find more information.

1. Go to www.factsurfer.com.
2. Enter "see a pineapple grow" into the search box and click 🔍.
3. Select your book cover to see a list of related content.

Index

The images in this book are reproduced through the courtesy of: Jiri Miklo, front cover (pineapple); yevgeniy11, front cover (young pineapple); gan chaonan, front cover (cutting); Davydenko Yuliia, p. 3; Crezalyn Nerona Uratsuji/ Getty Images, pp. 4-5; KevinKlimaPhoto, pp. 6-7; Purnananad Gogoi, pp. 8-9; Nakornthai, pp. 10-11; govindamadhava108, p. 11 (sandy soil); ESB Professional, p. 11 (heat and sunlight); Martin Valigursky, p. 11 (water); Anant Kasetsinsombut/ Alamy, pp. 12-13; Cristina linescu, pp. 14-15; asharkyu, pp. 16-17, 22 (ripe); Jes2u.photo, pp. 18-19; ARIES_Studio, p. 19 (cake); New Africa, p. 19 (juice); Nataly Studio, p. 19 (slices); Khumthong, pp. 20-21; Oliver Asselin/ Alamy, p. 22 (cuttings); Microgen, p. 22 (fuse); Sombat Muycheen, p. 22 (shipped); Pakhnyushchy, p. 22 (tropics); Viktar Malyshchyts, p. 23.